Getting Involved

A Guide to Student Citizenship

Mark Kann
Todd Belt
Gabriela Cowperthwaite
Steven Horn
University of Southern California

New York   San Francisco   Boston
London   Toronto   Sydney   Tokyo   Singapore   Madrid
Mexico City   Munich   Paris   Cape Town   Hong Kong   Montreal

ISBN 0-205-30933-X

Printed in the United States of America

10 9 8 7 6 5   03 02

Contents

Preface

The introductory American politics course at the University of Southern California is "The Theory and Practice of American Democracy." During the spring of 1998, Professor Mark Kann (with help from Richard Cone of the Joint Educational Project and Ann Crigler of the Unruh Institute) initiated a plan to augment the theory part of the course by requiring all students to "practice democracy." Gabriela Cowperthwaite, a graduate student coordinator, contacted community groups and political organizations willing to work with student teams for a 10-week period. When the fall 1998 semester arrived, graduate teaching assistants Todd Belt and Steven Horn organized students into teams, helped them to develop or select projects, and then guided them through their projects.

The four of us brought to the "practice democracy" project considerable experience with politics and political internships. Our political experience ranged from grassroots activism to campaign management. Two of us had covered politics for newspapers. All four had significant experience in placing students in political internships. Still, none of us had ever experimented with organizing so many students (100+) into teams that set goals, developed game plans, and implemented them within the span of one semester.

The experiment was a great success. Nearly 81% of student participants felt that the "practice democracy" project was a positive learning adventure. Some 12% expressed mixed feelings and only 7% felt that their time would have been better spent elsewhere. Importantly, many students lost their cynicism about politics and more than a few became enthusiasts for political participation.

This volume is a practical guide to student involvement in politics. It draws on our "practice democracy" project as well as our prior experience with politics and internships. The planning phase of the project was supported by the Corporation for National Service under Learn and Serve America Grant No. 97LHEWA042. The views in this booklet are those of the authors and do not necessarily reflect the position of the Corporation for National Service or the Learn and Serve America Program.

Becoming a Student Citizen 1

Exhilaration, Enlightenment, Expertise, and Empowerment

Why should you get involved in American politics? Why should you read the morning newspaper or watch the nightly news? Why should you discuss and debate seemingly irresolvable political issues? Why should you bother to vote on election day? Why should you become an active participant in American politics?

Many Americans do not get involved in politics. Some people say that they are more-or-less satisfied. Everything is all right. There is no particular need to follow politics, register to vote, or join interest groups and political organizations because life is just fine. These are politically contented Americans.

Other people choose not to get involved in politics because they are extremely dissatisfied. Social problems such as poverty and pollution are not being solved by the government. Business tycoons and dishonest politicians appear to govern the nation. These highly dissatisfied Americans are convinced that the common man and woman have little impact. After all, you can't fight city hall!

Still other Americans feel they have more important things to do than to consider, investigate, and confront the major political issues of the day. They need to study biology to get good grades. They must work long hours to pay the rent. Their love life is a complete mess. These Americans may feel that they should participate more in politics but, alas, their priorities preclude them from monitoring and molding public policy.

Notice however that millions and millions of Americans do get involved in politics. They keep up with current issues. They discuss and debate them among friends, neighbors, and co-workers. They register and vote in elections. They even participate in local organizations, interest groups, political parties, school boards, and government commissions that influence public decision making.

Furthermore, large numbers of college students throughout the nation are active in politics. They help to define campus issues and resolve campus problems, organize campus affiliates of interest groups and political organizations, and engage in off-campus activities that span the entire spectrum of political participation. Why do they get involved in politics? Why should you get involved in politics? Here are four reasons why you should become a student citizen: it can be exhilarating; it is often enlightening; it builds your expertise; and it empowers you to improve your campus, community, and nation.

Reason 1: Student Citizenship Can Be Exhilarating
Many of us think about political participation as a matter of licking envelopes, enduring long and dull speeches, reading thick reports and jargon-laden law books, or being deadened by number-crunching statistics. At the same time, we think about politics as an arena for dishonesty, deception, and disinformation. This is only part of the story.

Participating in politics often is exciting. Students who work on election campaigns may lick envelopes. But they also discuss important issues with colleagues and with potential voters; they sit in on policy meetings and planning sessions; they organize appearances for their candidates, attend fund-raisers, speak directly with local politicians, and even meet major national figures.

During the November 1998 national elections, for example, we had one team of students campaigning to elect Democratic party candidates. In the middle of the project, several of the students attended events where they met U.S. Senator Barbara Boxer, Vice President Al Gore, and President Bill Clinton. One student was especially animated when describing how he spent several hours one weekend "hanging out" with Secret Service agents.

Meeting public figures is stimulating. It gives you a sense of how it feels to be at the center of things. It enables you to speak to people who work behind the scenes as well as to people who appear in the newspapers and on the nightly news, make life and death decisions about crime and war, and lead the community or nation.

Perhaps less glamorous but possibly even more exhilarating, participating at the local level affords you a superb opportunity to have a discernible impact on people's lives in just a few weeks. If you get involved in developing a computer-training program for youths from low-income families, or in organizing a meeting to address dangerous traffic problems in the neighborhood, or in teaching a mini-civics course at a nearby high school, you help to enrich individual lives, solve significant problems, and inspire young people.

You know about mudslinging during elections. You have heard about the partisan wrangling in Congress. It is easy to be disenchanted with politicians and politics. However, we believe that the best kept "secret" about American politics is that being a part of it can be exhilarating! As a student citizen, you can rise above everyday complacency and cynicism to join in a public effort to make your campus or community or nation a better place to live and work. The effort can be as exciting as the outcome.

Reason 2: Student Citizenship Can Be Enlightening

Conventional classroom learning is important. Lectures, books, discussions, and case studies can teach you a great deal about democratic theories that set the standards for American politics and scholarly studies that describe and explain American politics. Usually, these lessons are based on other people's experiences. Missing are lessons based on your own experiences.

If you are like most students, you probably have little or no political experience. Although you may occasionally follow current events and even discuss political issues, your sustained interest in politics and your knowledge about politics are apt to be haphazard. Moreover, there is a good chance that you have not registered to vote or actually voted with any regularity. Also, you probably do not participate in the community organizations, interest groups, and public institutions that shape the course of American politics.

Becoming an experienced student citizen can be a wonderful adventure in learning. It can enrich and augment what you learn in the classroom; it can be a significant source of enlightenment.

A student who gets involved in politics is in a position to weigh what other people say against the student's own experiences. Suppose, for example, that your American government class is debating democratic ideals. Should American politics be judged by the standards of "participatory democracy" (whereby ordinary citizens discuss, debate, and decide major political issues) or by the standards of "representative democracy" (whereby ordinary citizens elect representatives and then rely on their representatives to discuss, debate, and decide major political issues)?

If you have no political experience, the debate will almost certainly be abstract. Your choice will likely be a matter of blind faith. If you are idealistic, you might assert that average citizens do have the capacity to deliberate and make wise decisions for themselves. If you are more skeptical, you may argue that ordinary citizens are too passionate, irrational, and impulsive to make wise decisions and should instead rely on elected leaders. If you are ambivalent, you may simply shrug your shoulders.

Becoming a student citizen will provide you with a reservoir of political experiences that helps to produce a more sophisticated understanding of American democracy. The "idealistic you" may participate in a project in which many people slack off and allow an energetic leader to carry the load. If so, you may become more sympathetic to representative democracy. The "skeptical you" may engage in a project in which members deliberate and make consensus decisions. Here, you may better appreciate the potential for participatory democracy. Finally, depending on your experience, the "ambivalent you" may conclude that a mix of participation and representation is best. Political experience can sensitize you to the subtleties of political understanding.

Importantly, becoming a student citizen will make politics seem more familiar to you. It gives you a view "from the ground up" that you are unlikely to get in lectures or books. For example, America's major national political parties tend to be invisible except every fourth year when they stage national conventions to nominate presidential and vice-presidential candidates. Nonetheless, most political party activity takes place year-round at the state and local levels, where you are likely to have an opportunity to participate.

Your involvement with local political parties should provide you first-hand knowledge about the large number of people and resources needed by candidates to get noticed, nominated, and elected. You may learn how party unity is restored after candidates compete against each other for their party's nomination. You may also begin to appreciate how many people volunteer their time, energy, and money simply because they are dedicated to party goals and public service. These are just a few of the important lessons you may learn from your participation in politics.

Reason 3: Student Citizenship Can Build Expertise
Participating in politics involves working with diverse people. As a student citizen, you may encounter individuals who agree with your goals, partly agree with them, generally disagree with them, or perhaps care little about them. Most people are likely to have different priorities.

You may interact with people of a different sex, religion, race, ethnicity, class, sexual orientation, age, and education. You may also collaborate with people from different language groups, countries, and cultures. You surely will be working with individuals who have diverse character traits. They may be honest or dishonest, responsible or irresponsible, committed or complacent, reliable or unreliable, and so forth.

One of the great challenges—and great opportunities—of political involvement is learning to work in a constructive way with many different kinds of people. To meet the challenge effectively, you must learn to develop some expertise in practical skills such as negotiation, compromise, and leadership. In turn, your mastery of these skills will be useful to you throughout your life.

Negotiation. Suppose you are working with a team of students to elect Candidate Z. You and the other volunteers may support Z for different reasons. Also, people on your team are likely to come from different backgrounds and bring varied skills and commitments to the campaign. A student citizen needs to figure out how to be effective under these circumstances. Ideally, you learn to identify and emphasize the common goals that bring co-workers together; ideally, you negotiate a division of labor that enables each individual to contribute in his or her own way. Importantly, you learn that the art of negotiation (very much like the art of politics) requires you to set aside your ego to ascertain the most effective way to achieve common goals.

Compromise. Sometimes teams of students cannot identify common ground. Instead of getting involved in a nonproductive conflict, you should learn to forge compromises. Suppose you are developing a flyer to announce Candidate Z's upcoming speech on campus. You may want to highlight Z's pro-choice position on abortion but your co-workers may insist that Z's position on welfare reform is more important. Lacking consensus, you learn to compromise, perhaps by putting both issues on the flyer or by agreeing to focus on a third issue that merits notice. Compromise is a skill. Politics is a wonderful arena for practicing it.

Leadership. Politics also is a superb arena for developing and practicing leadership skills. How do you inspire others to collaborate? How do you motivate them to put in the time, energy, and resources to get the job done? How do you prevent disputes and resolve conflicts? How do you provide recognition and reward for a job well done? You may have to learn the answer to these questions by trial and error; but you are also likely to work with people and politicians who model leadership skills. The opportunities to gain expertise in leadership are nearly unlimited in politics.

Becoming a student citizen also invites you to develop other sorts of expertise such as petitioning and protesting to articulate your viewpoint, marketing and public relations to disseminate your ideas, organizing and managing to build coordinated team efforts, and much more. In turn, your emerging expertise can empower you to be more effective in politics.

Reason 4: Student Citizenship Can Be Empowering

An essential element of democracy is that citizens govern themselves, directly or indirectly. Self-government assumes that citizens keep abreast of relevant information and make intelligent decisions. It requires them to voice their viewpoints through conversations, letters, petitions, proposals, and protests as well as through elections. That way, citizens can have a year-round impact on law and public policy, and on the legislators who make law and public policy. Thomas Jefferson believed that citizen participation is the foundation of American democracy.

Why is getting involved so crucial to democracy? Getting involved is probably the best way for you to understand how your own life, desires, interests, and goals are related to other people's lives, desires, interests, and goals. Whether you join neighbors in an effort to prevent a toxic waste dump from moving into your area or help to raise money for a statewide petition drive, political participation invites you to view yourself *in relationship to* other people. It gives you a better sense of the broad *American public* and the *public good.*

Some ethicists, scholars, and politicians believe that students (indeed, all Americans) have a moral obligation to engage in public service and seek the public good. If you willingly accept the many benefits of growing up in or living in our prosperous democratic society, then you should reciprocate by maintaining and improving that society. If you are disenchanted with the persistence of poverty and elitism in America, for example, then you should take an active role in seeking greater social justice and more democracy. A student citizen recognizes his or her obligation to serve the public good.

If you recognize and respect the obligations of citizenship, you may become dedicated to public service. You may realize that it is easy to complain about paying too much money in taxes, or suffering so much government inefficiency, or demanding more adequate public health care. However, it is far more difficult and daunting to face up to the complex dilemmas, trade-offs, and experiments that preoccupy people involved in political life.

Suppose you are working with a group of homeowners to persuade city government to fill in the potholes in city streets. You will quickly learn that it takes money to fill the potholes, that other citizens feel the money would be better spent on schools, and still others want the money for social measures such as subsidized pre-natal health care for low-income women. A student citizen who appreciates the dilemmas and trade-offs of American politics is likely to empower himself or herself by focusing on viable political options that may influence the outcomes.

Instead of shouting "hurrah" or "boo" on every issue of concern to you, the more sophisticated student citizen will seek out potential trade-offs and urge decision makers to develop "win-win" policies that may offer something to everyone but perhaps something less than what anyone desires. A student citizen can take great pride in engineering a partial victory that may be the basis for even greater achievements in the future.

One More Reason: It's Required

You may be in the position of becoming a student citizen because your professor is requiring you to gain first-hand political experience in an internship or team project. Or you may be getting involved in politics as an alternative to a term paper. Perhaps you have signed on for an extra-credit project. Maybe you are simply going along with friends. Whatever the motive, you are likely to find that taking an experimental attitude will serve you well.

We required our students to practice democracy. We recommended that they develop or select projects that best fit their own political predispositions and interests. We also invited them to see their involvement as an experiment in which they could "try on" different political personalities. A very shy student telephoned potential voters and found out what it was like to address the public. Another student who identified herself as a moderate Democrat worked on a Republican party campaign and, as a result, switched her party loyalty. Yet another student overcame his fear of computers by helping to construct a web page for his team.

Open yourself up to the experiment of American politics. Reflect on everything. Analyze each twist and turn. Transform obstacles into challenges. Talk things over with other students, team members, allies, professors, relatives, and friends. Every experience offers you an opportunity to learn. Your openness and reflection will draw to you the exhilaration, enlightenment, expertise, and empowerment that characterize so much of political engagement.

The rest of this booklet is a practical guide to assist you along the path of becoming a student citizen. It will help you to get connected to community and political organizations, foster teamwork, set goals and develop game plans, experiment with tactics, build alliances, anticipate obstacles, and make a difference on campus, in the community, and for the nation.

Getting Connected   2

Experimental Attitude, Self-Inventory, And Making Contact

A few of our students gleefully dived into political projects outside of the classroom. They wanted to make politics their career and student citizenship was a step that hastened them to their future. We had one student who aspired to become a U.S. Representative before she turned thirty. She chose to work on environmental issues. She was committed to improving the environment. But she also calculated that environmental issues would be important to her political platform down the line.

You may fit this profile. However, the chances are quite strong that you are not committed to a predetermined career in political life. How then do you decide on a project that will be interesting or valuable to you? And once you decide, how do you get involved with campus groups, community associations, or political organizations that are already practicing politics in your area of interest? How do you get connected so you can get started?

Experimental Attitude

Most students are not certain of their career goals. Few students strive for careers in politics. And many students have a tendency to change their minds. They may set out on one career path only to change direction several times. If this sounds like you, try to take an experimental attitude. Getting involved in politics may help you to tap some new interests, filter out a few prior options, and perhaps make a few valuable connections. You may end up like the student who volunteered to work with a local community group that was cleaning up graffiti and later started her own sandblasting company.

Whatever project you choose does not have to seem like a perfect fit. The perfect fit between person and politics rarely happens. Once you begin a project, any project, try to figure out ways to create responsibilities that relate to some of your interests or aspirations. Take some initiative. You may be in a position where you can effectively invent your own assignments or perhaps design your own way of completing an assignment.

Consider the student who interned at the local politics desk in the news division of a television station. She did some digging on her own and then pitched a story about campaign donations. She was quite persuasive. Her producer allowed her to refocus her internship and energies on researching this new topic for the station. Creating your own niche in an organization can be a challenging and rewarding experience.

If you open yourself to new experiences and try to make them work for you, you may discover some new things about yourself. For example, you may begin a project by designing a web page for a school district that wants to keep parents informed about its activities. In the process, you may discover that you are much less interested in designing the web page than in teaching school children how to access and use web pages.

With an experimental attitude, you will understand that the best choice for your political project may be to pick *something*. Try to develop a project that fits your interests; but also remember that virtually any political project offers the potential to be both interesting and valuable to you.

Self-Inventory

Your political project options may vary. Your professor may present you with a list of neighborhood organizations and local political campaigns and then require you to team up with other students to get some "real world" experience. That is what we did. However, you may be enrolled in a class that gives you the choice of doing a term paper or a political internship. Or you may walk past a bulletin board where a flyer about campus recycling catches your eye. Whatever your circumstances, you want to get connected with the option that best suits your personality and interests.

If your professor presents you with a list of organizations that are seeking student participants, or if you are willing to work with them, you need to evaluate the options for yourself. If your professor does not provide you with a list of options, you may need to develop your own political project. The search for the best option or the effort to create your own project can be great fun. Start digging.

Where? Inventory your own interests. Write down things that you like to do, things you find rewarding. Begin with the more personal questions, ones that only you can answer about yourself:

- Are you a people person?
- Would you like to have a mentor?
- Do you enjoy doing research on your own?
- What will it take to get you to wear a business suit?

- Are you comfortable with public speaking?

Next, inventory your skills. What can you do that may be helpful for your political involvement? Consider questions such as:

- Are you a good writer?
- Do you have advanced computer skills?
- Are you most productive in the A.M. or P.M.?
- Do you prefer to work in an office or "in the field"?
- Are you creative?

Finally, consider what issues make you stand up and take notice. Be aware of issues that strike you as "yawners." Ask yourself questions related to your choice of political projects:

- Are you interested in working on legal cases?
- Would you like to create a web site?
- Do race issues concern you?
- Are you irritated by trash in neighborhood parks?
- Do you enjoy political campaigns?

Your answers may suggest a number of political projects. If not, they should certainly help you to narrow your focus and better define your potential role as a student citizen. Remember this: whether you consider yourself to be a political person or not, there is a very strong chance that there are political projects out there that will resonate with important aspects of your life. You might be uncomfortable with political competition and conflict, for example, but you may find the challenge of organizing a public event (that happens to be political) quite thrilling!

Making Contact

Once you have defined your interests, start making contact. If you are working with a list of options, you need to contact the appropriate resource person, introduce yourself, and set up a meeting to clarify expectations. If you are developing your own project, you need to contact organizations that are already working in your field of interest. How do you do this?

Start with people who you already know. They are often the best contacts. Let family members, friends, neighbors, and teachers know that you are interested in ending gang violence or stopping drunk driving or freeing Tibet. Ask them if they know any people or organizations working in these areas. You may stumble across a friend who knows someone whose brother-in-law is involved in your area of interest. Get names and phone numbers and begin calling people. Even if your contacts cannot directly help you, they may know someone else who can.

Think of "key words" related to your area of interest. Then connect to the World Wide Web. Plug any word or word combination into a search engine and take down e-mail addresses and phone numbers of relevant organizations. Read newspaper articles related to your topic. Take note of people and groups that are quoted, interviewed, or discussed. If appropriate, contact them.

Scan the Yellow Pages. Select words related to your topic. Look them up. If you find appropriate groups, telephone them and let them know about your interest. They may be the right group or they may be able to put you in touch with the right organization.

Working From a Script

You may find it useful to create a script to use when addressing organization representatives. Here is a sample.

Hi, my name is Derek Wilson. I am a sophomore at the University of Southern California and I am interested in human rights. I would like to meet with someone in your organization to discuss internship or volunteer opportunities.

It is likely that the person with whom you need to speak will be out of the office. Try to get his or her name, extension, e-mail address, voice mail, or fax number. Leave a message:

Hi, my name is Derek Wilson. I am a sophomore at the University of Southern California and I am interested in human rights. I would like to speak with you about internship or volunteer opportunities. Please contact me at this phone number (give number) or e-mail address (give address). In the meantime, I will fax you my résumé.

Write a cover letter that reminds the contact person that you called, restates your desire to talk about an intern or volunteer position, and again provides your phone number and e-mail address. Then fax the cover letter and your résumé as soon as possible.

Be persistent. If you have not heard from the contact person after a few days, call again. Keep your messages clear and concise. Remind the person who you are, what your school is, your interest in their organization, and your desire for an intern or volunteer position. The contact person may be sufficiently impressed with your persistence to create a position just for you.

When you finally reach the contact person, continue to be clear and concise. Say what you desire. Don't be shy. You want a position but you are offering something extremely valuable in return: your time and energy. If the discussion indicates that some sort of position is possible, ask to arrange a face-to-face meeting to discuss your potential role in the organization. You may want to ask some basic logistical questions. Where are you located? Is parking available? Are you available in the late afternoon?

A face-to-face meeting will help you to assess the people you would be working with, perhaps the work environment, and the nature of your responsibilities. It is also an opportunity to talk about "the big picture." What is the organization's overall mission? Does it have a mission statement? How will your role as an intern or volunteer help the organization achieve its goals? How can the organization help you to achieve your goals? Be honest and open about your interests. Be prepared to discuss your personal strengths and weaknesses.

The good news is that most people enjoy helping students. If your interests coincide with an organization's goals and activities, there is a good chance that they will find a place for you, or perhaps help you to find intern or volunteer opportunities elsewhere. Indeed, an energetic young person who displays initiative and perseverance in the cause of doing good deeds is awfully hard to resist. Make yourself irresistible.

Avoiding Desperation

What should you do if you do not thrive on an experimental attitude, remain unsure about your interests, and do not receive a positive response (or any response) from contact people and organizations? Don't feel desperate. You still have options.

Remember, there are endless choices for student citizens to get involved in politics. There are often state, county, and city political campaigns that are getting started or are in the works that afford volunteers a chance to gain some valuable political experience. There are innumerable public officials working on the entire spectrum of political issues who desire interns to supplement their inadequate staffs. They offer you the possibility of working on issues ranging from street maintenance to street crime.

Meanwhile, major public interest groups such as the Sierra Club or Greenpeace have many opportunities for student volunteers. Public schools generally desire college student help that may focus on anything from tutoring individual students to lobbying the state legislature. Also, diverse communities generally host organizations that seek volunteers to help them support the rights and solve the problems of particular populations.

Many students like to work in organizations involved in the criminal justice system. Students who plan to go to law school, for example, often want to intern in law firms. We have had a mixed experience here. Some student interns end up doing routine clerical work that provides them little contact with the law or litigation. Others, however, are given challenging research assignments and opportunities to sit in on depositions and court hearings. Note that there are other criminal justice options that may result in highly rewarding experiences. You might consider working with local police departments that have programs to keep kids in school, away from drugs, and out of gangs.

Churches and charitable organizations often need assistance with food and clothing drives, soup kitchens, and homeless shelters. They are always looking for the assistance of dependable people.

Should all else fail, remember that other students may be working on projects already. Talk to them. Find out what they are doing. And then explore whether it is possible for you to team up with one of them or join an ongoing team.

If this does not work out, find something on campus. Most college campuses have "issue groups" concerned with causes related to the environment, human rights, and other topics. They often have "identity groups" that promote traditions, values, and goals associated with Asian Americans, Gays and Lesbians, and so forth. Finally, they usually have political groups such as Young Republicans, Campus Democrats, Libertarians, and more. Find out what they are doing and sign up for one of their activities.

A democracy provides endless opportunities for student citizenship. While the options are multifaceted and complex, your challenge is actually quite simple: find a project and get started!

Building Teamwork 3

Participation, Leadership, Buying In, and Team Dynamics

Whether you get connected to an individual internship or a group project, you will be working with other people. Building teamwork among those people will be crucial to your success.

You may find yourself working with individuals who share a strong cooperative ethic. You may end up on a team dominated by one or two strong personalities. Or maybe the particular mix of co-participants and social skills distributed among you may defy easy description.

Be self-conscious about how you organize relationships with co-participants. Good teamwork can make your project pleasant, effective, educational, and satisfying. A lack of teamwork, on the other hand, can be immensely frustrating.

Two Models of Teamwork

More likely than not, the relationship between you and your co-participants will be determined by your particular mix of personalities. If most involved individuals are energetic, interested, responsible, and committed to the project, you may find that the PARTICIPATORY MODEL of teamwork is most suitable for you. The participatory model invites all team members to take part in deliberations and decision making. It strives for all final decisions to be made by informal group consensus rather than by formal voting and majority rule.

Here are several advantages to the participatory model. First, the more that all members of your group are engaged in the project, the more likely that they will contribute good ideas and suggestions. Ideally, all team members will feel free to offer their own thoughts. Second, a participatory team is more apt to recognize and utilize the strengths of each member. Without a clearly defined leader, each member may take the lead in different aspects of the project. Finally, this model invites each member to take initiative during the project and allows all members to feel an equal sense of accomplishment at the end of the project.

On the other hand, you may find that some team members feel more comfortable taking a passive role by allowing one or more individuals to take charge, lead discussions, determine goals, develop game plans, and select tactics. This situation is likely to occur when one powerful personality comes to dominate the group. It is also likely to happen when one individual has a lot more political experience than everyone else. In this instance, you may want to consider a LEADERSHIP MODEL of teamwork.

What are the advantages of the leadership model? First, it saves time. All team members do not have to deliberate and debate every small and large issue. Instead, the leader will resolve minor disputes and even make the major decisions regarding the project. That way, the team can get on with the project as soon as possible. Second, it is possible that the most experienced member of the team is the most qualified to make team decisions. Such a leader may be able to identify dead-ends, make appropriate contacts, and choose the most effective tactics to get the job done. Finally, an effective leader can help to prepare other team members to be future leaders. Once you see what it takes to be an effective leader, you may decide to step forward on the next project.

Note that both models invite considerable flexibility. The participatory model gives priority to deliberation and consensus, but it does not preclude authorizing one team member or another to take the lead in different aspects of the project. Similarly, the leadership model tends to work best when the leader strives to get all team members as involved in deliberation and decision making as possible. Your best guide to collaboration may be common sense.

Getting to Know Each Other

When you first meet team members, exchange telephone numbers, e-mail addresses, and rough schedules. Decide on convenient meeting times and begin to make the decisions necessary for getting your project going. Simultaneously, begin to familiarize yourself with the strengths and skills that each team member brings to the project. Does one person stand out as a speaker? Does another student write particularly well? Who is the computer expert in the group? Is there an artist among you? Perhaps most important, has anyone had significant political experience? By learning each other's strengths and skills as well as preferences, you position yourself to help the team achieve its maximum potential.

Of course, the members on your team may not possess every skill needed to complete your project. Perhaps you have a friend or know of an organization that can provide some help. Be aware, however, that team members may have to assume responsibilities that require them to learn a new skill or engage in an unfamiliar activity. This journey into the "unlearned and unknown" may be the most exciting and educational aspect of student citizenship.

Remember, taking an experimental attitude is probably the best way to benefit under these circumstances. Put aside the urge to say "I can't speak in public," or "I don't know how to construct a web page." Sometimes you need to be bold. Figure out what you ought to do, take a chance, and see what happens. You may surprise yourself.

Key Questions for Success

• How much time can team members devote to the project?

• What skills and experience are needed for the project?

• What resources are available?

• Can the team call on outside people or organizations to augment its skills and resources?

• Are team members willing to try something new?

• How can each member contribute to the team's success?

Buying-In

One essential ingredient of successful teamwork is the "buy-in." If everyone on your team is excited about the project and convinced that it is worth his or her time, effort, and energy, you are likely to accomplish a great deal and achieve a considerable degree of satisfaction. That is why it is important for team members to discuss what it is about the project that initially interested them and why they think the project is significant. Hesitant participants may buy-in when they listen to other students talk about their motivation and evaluation of the collaborative project.

In our American government class, we invited students to form teams that either (1) developed their own political projects or (2) selected from a predetermined list of projects. Most students formed teams that selected projects from our list. They thought that some of the options were more attractive than others and chose them immediately. The list quickly shrunk. A few indecisive students complained that the remaining projects were uninteresting. They felt that they had been "stuck" with lousy choices.

Clearly, it is desirable to work on a project that interests and excites you. Nonetheless, if you feel that you have been "stuck" with a project, make the best of your situation. Figure out ways to make it interesting and important to you. See if other team members find it more challenging. Try to assume team responsibilities that may interest or challenge you regardless of the precise nature of the project. In other words, think about buying-in anyway.

Even when you buy in, you may discover that one or more of your co-participants are unmotivated. All they see is a burdensome requirement that must be fulfilled to pass the course. They make it clear that they are only willing to do the minimum necessary to complete the assignment. You may find such people frustrating, especially if you are to receive one team grade for the project. You worry that the unmotivated will drag your grade down or that you will have to do all the work while the lazy students get the same grade as you.

We found that the teams that achieved the most successful results got the best grades. Those who had the most fun were the ones that decided very early in the project that they would commit themselves not just to doing the minimum required but to making a difference in the community or in an election campaign. One student became so involved in his team project that he ultimately decided that he wanted to pursue a career in politics. You may find this kind of devotion is infectious. If a few team members are excited and committed, the unmotivated may be transformed into enthusiasts.

Of course, no amount of enthusiasm will move some students. You may encounter a team member who does next to nothing but is still willing to take credit for what other people do. The person who does nothing but tags along is commonly considered a "free rider." If your team has a free rider, do not give up on him easily. Perhaps all he needs is encouragement. Try to give him an easy first task to complete. That might give him some momentum. You may be tempted to chide, criticize, or even condemn a team member for slacking off. While team pressure is sometimes effective, keep in mind that this tactic may make the errant team member resentful and even less likely to help the group.

Our student teams reported that some of the least interested members at the beginning of the project gradually got more and more involved in the project. A few of them became the most active and enthusiastic participants by the project's end.

We had one small team in which only two members made a serious effort to conduct and complete a voter registration project. The two participants worked hard and long, and they developed a strong resentment of their team's free riders. One student explained:

> When our group was first set up, we had four members including myself. Jenny . . . became the other significant member of the group. However, John, who I have not heard from in a month, and Jerry, who may not even have a last name for all I know, did not help out at all. Jerry only decided that he would start participating about four or five days ago, considering that the final team paper for the project was due very shortly.

It may prove impossible to eliminate the free-rider problem altogether. At the very least, recognizing the problem should help you to appreciate and understand an important obstacle in democracy: not every citizen is willing to fulfill his or her civic duties (such as paying taxes, voting, performing jury duty, or serving in the military). As a last resort, you may want to consult with your professor.

Keep·in mind that the more that you and other team members take a positive approach to the project, the more likely that every team member will buy into it, generate enthusiasm, participate, and contribute fully to the team effort. We had one team in which everyone pitched in. Still, the team fell a bit short of accomplishing its main goal (to produce and promote a public-service pamphlet). Our students were so enthusiastic about their success in building teamwork that they were only modestly disappointed when their contact person for promoting the pamphlet proved to be too busy to meet with them or even talk to them.

Team Dynamics

Do not be surprised if disagreements among team members surface from time to time. Individuals' political views and priorities differ, so do their preferences and tolerance for other people's idiosyncrasies. Conceivably, every co-participant will have a slightly different idea of what needs to be done or even what counts as success. Be aware that it is probably a good thing if team members care enough about these issues to argue about them. That means they have bought in. Now the challenge is to deal with disagreements in ways that protect and promote team effectiveness.

We had one student team working on a project to promote human rights. It faced a substantial challenge. During initial meetings, team members were quite congenial. Individuals got along with each other and moved steadily toward accomplishing team goals. After all, everyone is for human rights. Right? Alas, the project quickly moved into a controversial phase.

The students had to designate the specific rights that the team would advocate. One student proposed a universal right to health care. Another student argued for the right to a living wage. However, several conservative team members claimed that these were either "economic rights" or "no rights at all." They certainly were not human rights. The conservatives wanted to focus instead on free speech and voting rights.

How did our student citizens resolve this disagreement? Good team dynamics. Team members expressed their differences without personalizing them or antagonizing other team members. Next, they decided to search for those human rights on which they could all agree and then compromise their differences. This enabled them to get past their debate and get on with their project.

If you encounter serious team disagreements, our advice is to initiate a search for common ground. You have a limited amount of time for your project and can expect to accomplish only modest goals within the constraints of a semester or quarter. You need to make timely decisions even if you are not completely satisfied with them. If you feel very strongly about an issue but cannot convince other team members to do what you think is best, be flexible. Remember that you are always free to pursue your ideas at another time and place. Meanwhile, you can still participate in a useful experience that will likely improve your ability to advocate your position on the issue in the future.

You may be part of a team of student citizens that affiliates itself with a larger, more established organization. In this case, you and your team members may have to alter or even discard some of your original goals to participate effectively with people who have been working on "your issue" long before you got involved with it. This can be a frustrating experience.

We had one student team working with a community organization that sought to get the owner of an apartment complex for senior citizens living on fixed incomes to lower tenants' rents. Student team members had visions of conducting public protests, staging media events, and creating spectacles intended to pressure the owner into lowering rents. However, the students were told by the community organization that their plans were not "prudent." The community organization preferred a more measured approach.

The students' energy and enthusiasm for passionate, populist protests fizzled! Team members were a bit disheartened because they felt like they had volunteered to work with an organization that was paralyzed by inaction rather than propelled by heartfelt civic goals. Nonetheless, the students did learn an important lesson about the politics of change: it is often a very, very slow process.

To avoid being swallowed whole by a large, established organization, think about how your team can achieve its goals by working within the confines set by a partner organization. Do not give the impression that you have arrived on the scene to save the world or that your college-bred ideas are better than your partner's plans. However, do not be afraid to ask probing questions or to make suggestions, particularly related to your team's activities. Sometimes, the new perspective that you bring to an issue can help to re-energize an organization that has fallen into dull routine. Strive to work out a compromise that is acceptable to your team members and your partner organization.

Flexibility

Whether your team structure more closely approximates the participatory model or the leadership model, maintaining members' effort, energy, and enthusiasm may require considerable flexibility. A participatory team may harbor a student who is quiet at first, then leads by example, and finally takes the initiative to encourage other members to do their jobs. On the other hand, team members may discover the group's success is contingent on a quiet individual who functions as a "dependable rock." He just plugs away, even during moments when others are paralyzed by frustration.

Conversely, a leader-based team may develop a division of labor that relies on individual members to do their jobs without any external prodding or supervision. In this instance, the wise leader might back off, perhaps offer her help, but ultimately "empower" each member to take responsibility for their part of the project. As in democracy, when people feel their ideas and actions make a difference, they are more likely to participate in effective ways.

Flexibility is especially important when team members generate disagreements and conflicts. Remember, it is okay to disagree respectfully. But it also should be a priority to resolve disagreements in ways that help the team to accomplish its goals. Sometimes, you need to recognize the wisdom of putting away your ego to enable the group to accomplish its goals.

Many of the student citizens who participated in our team projects encountered mild disagreements among themselves as well as with their contact organizations. They generally understood that part of the challenge of getting involved in politics is figuring out ways to resolve disagreements in order to accomplish worthwhile goals. And with very few exceptions, the students' completion of their team projects and the accomplishment of their goals resulted in a deep sense of personal pride and accomplishment.

You may even get a bonus payoff. Many of our students remarked that they developed a strong sense of camaraderie among team members. One student reported that his co-participants celebrated the successful completion of their team project by singing along with Bob Marley on a car radio. He was confident that his newfound friendships would last well beyond the class.

Planning Participation 4

Goals, Game Plans, and Plan B

You feel ready to go. You are connected to a project. You are part of a team. Is it time for you to dive right in? Not quite. Consider these questions. Do you have a clear idea of what you want to accomplish? Do you have a strategy for achieving success? Do you have a sense of the likely outcome of your efforts?

It is important to plan your participation. You should select specific goals and be prepared to negotiate your goals with other team members, project supervisors, or perhaps your partner organization. You should develop a game plan by brainstorming and choosing among the alternative possibilities for achieving your goals. You should consider a Plan B just in case something goes wrong. Planning participation now will enable you to focus your energies and be more effective later.

Choosing Goals

Having selected a project (and perhaps a team), you should specify your main goal or goals. Sometimes this will be easy. If you are working on Candidate Z's campaign, your likely goal is to elect Candidate Z. Sometimes, however, specifying goals is a bit more complex. If you are helping to set up a public forum on problems with local trash collection, your goals may be to fill all of the seats in the auditorium, organize an informative program, publicize a problem, and promote a particular viewpoint. Be clear on your main goal or goals. Meanwhile, remember that you cannot accomplish everything in a short time.

Achieving clarity on your main goal or goals may be complicated by the fact that you are a member of a team. Can you articulate overall team goals even though individual members may have different ideas and priorities? Furthermore, can you negotiate a division of labor that enables the team to be effective in achieving its main goals but also allows individual members to pursue their pet priorities?

A further challenge may arise if you are working with a community group or political organization that has its own goals, priorities, and preferences. Will you (and team members) be in a position to retain your goals and still work with an organization that has different goals? Is there any possibility of negotiating a compromise that allows your team to retain its priorities and still contribute to a joint project with the partner organization?

Creativity can help you to sort out these complications. Consider this example. We had a team of student citizens working with the Democratic party to re-elect Barbara Boxer to the U.S. Senate. At first glance, it appeared that our students' main goal was to help re-elect the Senator, which was also the priority of the Democratic party. The problem was that one of our student citizens, Mike, was a dyed-in-the-wool Republican who actually supported Senator Boxer's opponent.

Why did this young Republican join a team devoted to campaigning for a Democrat? Mike joined the team because he had friends on it. He also wanted to learn more about campaigns. And he did not especially like the other team options. How then did Mike, his team, and the California Democratic party work out their differences?

Mike volunteered to research the Republican challenger's platform and track his campaign speeches and appearances. That way, Mike was able to fulfill several of his personal goals. Simultaneously, he contributed to the team effort by keeping members informed of opposition activities. That information enabled the team to be more effective in its efforts to support the Democratic party campaign for Senator Boxer's re-election.

Negotiating Goals

Whether you are an individual intern assigned to an ongoing operation or a team member working with a campus organization, community group, or political association, you will need to reconcile your own goals with other people's goals. Our advice is to set up a face-to-face meeting with your partner organization early in the project to clarify expectations.

Before you meet, explore the political terrain. Who are the players? What events have taken place? Have there been conflicts pertinent to your project? What has your partner organization done to date? The more you know, the better positioned you are to negotiate a project that respects your own goals and priorities.

For example, if you seek to reduce tensions between the police and homeless people in the area, search out recent newspaper articles related to the issue at the local library. If you will be working on a political campaign, read campaign materials for (and against) your issue or candidate. If your project involves working with a human rights organization, learn the organization's goals and recent activities. Once you familiarize yourself with the terrain, figure out ways to reconcile your goals with your partner's goals.

One student citizen, Susan, participated in a project which had the overall goal of informing neighborhood residents about a new development that was likely to increase traffic congestion in the neighborhood. Susan hoped to work directly with residents but her partner organization wanted her to sit in an office, design a flyer, and mail it to residents. After acquainting herself with the local scene, Susan suggested to her supervisors that a door-to-door information campaign followed by a presentation to a neighborhood council was an effective way to get out the message. Susan negotiated a compromise that enabled her to fulfill her goals by interviewing residents and speaking at a council meeting.

Negotiating Your Goals

This is a sample face-to-face first meeting between Angela and her intern supervisor, Barry. Notice how Angela gets her way.

Angela: *Hi, I'm Angela Johnson. I know that you must be busy with the food drive. I am a sophomore at City College. I am looking for some "real world" experience.*

Barry: *Hi, Angela. Let me be direct. We get a lot of interested students but they usually don't last. They lack "follow through."*

Angela: *I understand. Someone leaving halfway through a project can be troublesome. But that's not me. Here is a résumé that shows that I always give 110 percent.*

Barry: *Why are you interested in working at our shelter?*

Angela: *I researched local shelters. This shelter is close to school. Also, it caters to single mothers and their children. I am interested in the rights of homeless women and children. I eventually hope to practice law in this area.*

Barry: *Sounds good. You seem to be a responsible person. Can you start at noon on Monday? Perhaps you can help to organize our food drive. By the way, how did you know about the food drive?*

When you meet with someone from your partner group, treat the meeting as if it is a job interview. Pay attention to your dress and demeanor. Be on time. Listen to what the person wants or expects from you. Make eye contact. Ask about your partner's goals and priorities. What does your partner want to accomplish? Where does the organization need assistance? What can you do to help? People in community groups often feel that student participants are not particularly interested in their mission. This is an opportunity for you to stand out. Explain what drew you to the organization. Be practical. Show how your own goals and priorities complement their mission. Be flexible. Develop reasonable expectations that will enable you to fulfill your goals but also contribute to your partner organization's mission.

Develop Reasonable Expectations
After you identify your main goal or goals, think through expectations for your project. Consider your time frame. How much time can you and other team members contribute each week? How many weeks will you be involved? Within this time frame, realistically, how close do you think you can come to achieving your goals?

Our experience is that students usually underestimate the amount of time it takes to achieve even modest goals. Here are two rules of thumb:

- Your project is probably going to require more time than you think.

- There is a good chance that you will accomplish something less than you desire.

The point is not to give up before you start or even to scale back your expectations. Rather, from the outset, be modest. Try to develop a fairly accurate estimation of the relationship between your time investment and the likely payoff. That way, you have an excellent chance of experiencing the sense of accomplishment that comes with completing a project (rather than the sense of disappointment that comes with stopping short).

Next, you need to make some priority decisions. Surely you want to accomplish your main goals. But you may have other factors to consider. How important is it for you to learn a new skill? Do you aspire to network with people who may write you a letter of recommendation or help you attain future employment? Are you looking for a mentor? Are you seeking an interesting challenge or looking forward to working with a group of friends? Be prepared to reconcile your project goals with your personal priorities.

Keep in mind that your personal priorities may not mesh neatly with your team or with a partner organization. You may have to make some trade-offs. For example, your desire to learn how to create a web page will probably seem irrelevant to a team effort aimed at drumming up support for a community meeting next week. Perhaps you can learn some quick and easy Internet skills to develop an attractive flyer to distribute to local residents. Or, your wish to network with important people may be restrained by a partner organization that wants you to answer phones from an isolated location. If you recognize your own priorities and identify your partner organization's goals, you may be able to suggest an assignment that will place you in a busier political intersection.

Designing a Game Plan

Armed with explicit goals and reasonable expectations, you are ready to design your game plan, that is, your strategy for achieving your goals and fulfilling your expectations. This is a wonderful time for brainstorming.

Write down a few approaches to achieving your goals. Discuss them with team members. Seek ideas from parents, friends, local leaders, and others who may be acquainted with relevant matters. Consult your partner organization. The more people you talk to, the more possibilities you will have to consider. Once you have a sense of your options, it is usually helpful to think big but narrow your focus. Let us provide an example.

Suppose your main goal is to reduce the amount of gang activity in the local area. One possible game plan might involve helping young people to get out of gangs. Another game plan might focus on preventing young people from joining gangs. If the prevention approach interests you, then think about different ways to steer kids away from gangs. Perhaps you could educate them about the dangers of gang life. Or you might consider developing a safe alternative to gangs.

What kinds of alternatives? Again, brainstorm ideas. Ask others. But begin to focus in on practical measures. One of our student teams designed a game plan for reducing gang activity that focused on developing an after-school basketball league through a local church. Once that decision was made, our student citizens confronted a host of practical questions. What was the track record of other after-school programs? How could they get young people interested in their league? How often would teams play? Who would referee? Would there be awards? What should be done if fights break out? Notice that our students moved from the big abstract question of reducing gang activity to a series of narrow questions about their practical activities.

You also need to gauge ahead of time your likelihood of success. Continuing the example, our students consulted with local schools, parents, and community organizations to see if there was much need or demand for a basketball league. They solicited permission to use a local gymnasium. They planned to serve as the first referees but then cultivate a group of local teens to become the permanent referees.

In summary, you need to design a game plan that is consistent with your goals, that is narrow enough to accomplish in a relatively short time span, and that takes into account those factors that affect the project's success. That said, recognize that the best imaginable game plan cannot take into account all contingencies. The unexpected may occur and, suddenly, your game plan may become problematic (if not useless). Prepare yourself for the unexpected by having ready a back-up plan, Plan B.

Plan B

What should you do when something goes wrong? Your game plan may encounter serious obstacles. Our team of student citizens was quite excited when lots of kids showed up to enroll in their basketball league. But they were quite disappointed the next week when only a handful of kids appeared for the first basketball games. They organized a league with four teams but barely had enough players to make up one team.

This is the point at which you need to consider a back-up plan. One option is to salvage your original game plan by making some adjustments. In the example, our student citizens might have tried to do another sign-up event, switch from 5-person to 3-person teams, or perhaps transform the league into a basketball clinic.

Another option is to rethink and revise your game plan. Recall your original goals. Suppose you intern in a law office. Originally, you wanted to learn about the legal profession and get an attorney to write you a recommendation when you apply to law school. Suppose further that your game plan was to become so helpful to the attorneys that they would invite you to help research legal briefs, sit in on depositions, and attend court hearings. Finally, suppose instead that the intern coordinator assigns you to odd jobs such as answering phones, making copies, walking documents from here to there, stuffing envelopes, and so forth. How might you rethink and revise your game plan?

Aspects of your assignment may bring you into contact with people who could educate you about the legal profession. By being timely, cooperative, industrious, and perhaps inquisitive, you may impress the attorneys sufficiently so that they would be likely to write you letters of recommendation. Also, by asking if there are other ways for you to contribute to the firm, or by taking the initiative to volunteer for interesting activities, or by requesting to attend a hearing, you may be able to realize your original goals by altering your game plan.

If you feel that your game plan cannot be revised in suitable ways, it may be time to construct a new one. Perhaps you want to help preserve a healthy environment but your team project with the Sierra Club does not work out. Brainstorm other options. Consider partnering with different environmental groups. Think through game plans that may provide you great autonomy to do what you think best. But remember, time is short. Make sure that you do not spend all your time thinking about getting involved; devote most of your time to being involved.

The End Game

Getting involved in politics may be a lifelong endeavor for you. Getting involved as a class project, however, has a beginning, a middle point, and an end. Here are a few things to keep in mind as you anticipate implementing and completing your game plan.

If at any time during your project you feel discontented, try to keep your feelings at bay. Do not let your discontent be reflected in poor quality work, absenteeism, and other forms of shirking. Indeed, work on your project to the very best of your ability even if it includes lots of mindless, trivial tasks.

One reason why you should contain your discontent and maintain your work ethic is that you may be able to better your situation within the context of your current project or partnership. You may be able to switch teams. Perhaps you can change supervisors. Maybe you can revise your schedule. You are in the best position to improve your situation if the people with whom you work respect your positive attitude, admire your commitment, and appreciate your accomplishments.

Another reason for subduing your discontent is that you always want to be in a position to make a graceful exit. Whether you are constructing a new game plan or concluding a project, it is best to appreciate the opportunities and experiences that you have had (rather than to dwell on the negative personalities and nasty problems that plagued you). You may have learned to organize a precinct walk or publicize a community meeting. Even game plans that do not succeed can teach you important lessons.

Finally, think about the future. You never know who might be helpful (or harmful) to you tomorrow. Nor do you know who you might encounter in your future roles as family member, neighbor, worker, and citizen. If you develop good working relationships with people today, especially with those you find difficult, you are able to leave an organization or conclude a project knowing that you have acquired contacts that may someday prove beneficial to you.

Selecting Tactics 5

Options for Actions

With your goals and game plan decided, you must now select options among a range of tactics. What are tactics? They are the actions that you perform when following your game plan. For example, if your game plan is to raise public awareness about government waste (to achieve the goal of promoting a more limited government), you might consider using tactics such as distributing flyers, setting up information tables, or writing letters to local newspapers. Choosing goals and designing game plans involve thinking about politics; selecting tactics is about doing politics.

Tactics differ in important ways. Some tactics complement each other. Doing one often makes the other easier. Some tactics are more useful for carrying out your game plan than others. Some tactics may be inaccessible because you lack the time or resources to carry them out. This chapter considers tactics that are likely to be useful for you. It then discusses how you choose the ones that are most appropriate for your particular project.

Tactical Options

Tactics may serve multiple goals. For example, passing out flyers can serve the dual purpose of raising people's awareness about a particular issue and promoting a public letter-writing campaign to influence legislators. When selecting tactics, the question that you should always keep in mind is: "How does this tactic help me to implement my game plan?"

Doing Research. Doing research before, during, and after your involvement on any issue can be quite important. Research can uncover potential allies and opponents. It can help you to gauge what tactics have the highest chance of success. It can help you to evaluate the degree of your success.

The cost of doing research is usually minimal. Access to a telephone and a library may be sufficient. Although research may take some time, many individuals and groups have found that the

Internet provides a relatively quick vehicle for locating many types of information and organizations.

One of our teams discovered that research was particularly helpful for implementing its game plan, which was to set up a community meeting to discuss nuisance crimes around local liquor stores. Their research consisted of some library work, telephoning local groups, and door-to-door interviewing. Their payoff was that they were able to identify key individuals on both sides of the issue (discontented residents versus liquor store owners) who they later invited to their community meeting.

Written Material.   Another tactic involves developing, distributing, and/or posting written material on an issue you have chosen to address. Written material includes flyers, pamphlets, newsletters, and posters. The costs vary depending on quality of paper, format, and quantity.

Begin with an idea that has broad appeal. Try to make your material striking so that people will notice it. At the same time, make it appealing to the eye so that people will not be repulsed by it. Go for simplicity over detail. Most people want to digest data quickly and effortlessly. Be brief. Keep your print large. Slogans and symbols can be helpful for summarizing your main point.

Once you have designed and printed your written material, consider your options for distributing it. You can mail it, leave it on automobile windshields, post it on kiosks, hand it out to people in heavily trafficked zones, give it out door-to-door, or pass it out from an information table situated in a busy location.

One of our student teams working on a political campaign figured out that they could distribute a considerable amount of campaign material by scheduling talks at fraternity and sorority houses that were all located within a two-block area. At each stop, they distributed campaign information and bumper stickers.

Be aware that campuses and cities often have rules with respect to passing out flyers and other written material. Be sure to inform yourself about the legality of your actions before undertaking them. Contact your Student Affairs office or the local City Clerk's office to learn the rules.

Information Tables.   Information tables can be set up in heavily trafficked areas (such as outside of supermarkets) and at major public events (such as political rallies). It is often helpful to drape a banner over the front of the table to alert passers-by to the nature of your cause.

Some of our teams reported that having written materials available along with a "sign-up" sheet was useful for passing out information and contacting people who wanted further information. Setting up an information table is relatively inexpensive. It can serve multiple purposes. In addition to distributing information, it can be used to collect signatures for petitions, recruit volunteers, and solicit contributions.

As with passing out written materials, various policies and laws restricting the use of information tables vary from campus to campus, and from jurisdiction to jurisdiction. Learn the rules before you proceed.

Electronic Material.   The Internet offers tremendous opportunities for the dissemination of information in three ways. First, the World Wide Web offers you the opportunity to make information available to the public. But it does have drawbacks. Some of our teams discovered that it was difficult to get people to "stumble" across their web sites. If you plan to create a web site, you also must consider how to publicize your web site.

Second, Internet newsgroups provide you the opportunity to distribute information to targeted audiences. Newsgroups are electronic bulletin boards. They have a specific topic and users post information and comments on them. You may be able to find several different newsgroups associated with the issues at the core of your project.

A third way to distribute information is through electronic mail, or e-mail. While e-mail is quick and easy to use, be sure that you send information to individuals who you *know* are willing recipients. It is considered bad form to send a mass e-mail message to people you do not know. Also, be aware that people can often be contacted through list servers, which constitute e-mail's version of newsgroups.

The Internet can be an inexpensive way to reach people once the initial costs of the computer and access have been paid. Fortunately, both computer access and Internet access are free to most college students on most campuses. Certainly the Internet can be helpful for your project, but it probably should not constitute all of your efforts.

Phone Banks.   Another way to spread information about events, candidates, and issues is to contact people over the telephone. When several people make calls from several telephones, they are working a phone bank.

Start with an appropriate list of names and telephone numbers for your project. "Cold calling" or "random digital dialing" often proves ineffective. A good technique is to identify yourself early in the conversation and stress that you are not a salesperson. Also, give the person that you call an opportunity to state his or her opinion on the matter, ask questions, or respond to questions. That helps to draw them into the conversation.

A Sample Telephone Conversation

Below is a sample telephone conversation between a student citizen and a local resident.

Student: *Hello, my name is Pat and I was hoping to get a few minutes of your time to discuss the plight of the Spotted Owl in the Pacific Northwest. I am not selling anything or asking for a donation. May I ask you a few questions?*

Resident: *Well, I guess so, but I need to pick up my daughter in a few minutes.*

Student: *Thank you, I will be brief. First, are you familiar with the Spotted Owl?*

Resident: *No. I hunt but I've never seen one. I usually shoot pheasant.*

Student: *Well, sir, if you do see one, I certainly hope you don't shoot it. You see, it is on the endangered species list. There are just a few thousand left in the world.*

Resident: *Well, what do you want me to do about it?*

Student: *First, I would hope that you would become informed and tell others about it. Second, I encourage you to write a letter to your Congressional representatives to express your concern. Finally, if you are so inclined, we would love to have you volunteer to work with our group to save this species.*

Resident: *Well, I don't know. Doesn't protecting this or that species get in the way of development and cost people their jobs?*

Student: *That is not always the case. . . .*

The best time to catch people at home is between 6:00 P.M. and 8:00 P.M. While staffing phone banks is labor intensive, it can be very effective if a list of contacts has been compiled carefully and long distance fees are avoided or minimized.

When telephoning people, be prepared for them to be too busy or too uninterested to speak with you. Also, you may get rude remarks and hang-ups. Remember to remain calm and kind. It is not personal. Many people do not like to receive unsolicited phone calls and react accordingly.

Fundraising. Fundraising is a vital part of most political activity. It is done in a number of ways, including door-to-door campaigns, charging admission to special events, and telephone and mail solicitations. Fundraising requires time, energy, and patience (as well as an ability to tolerate criticism).

If you wish to experiment with fundraising, learn the rules and restrictions on your campus or in your local jurisdiction. Once you understand your options, think through your campaign. Be prepared to say why people should donate money to your cause (as opposed to any other cause). Work up a list of potential and likely contributors. Set a fundraising goal. Then see what you can achieve in a short period.

Petitioning. Petitioning can be an effective tool for getting attention from legislators, government agencies, important organizations, or targeted corporations. Petitions should be short statements which request that a particular policy or action be implemented, halted, or changed. If many signatures are attached to a petition, it can generate significant notice.

When you collect signatures, be certain not to mislead people. Be clear on your issue. Let them know what action you advocate. Tell them to whom the petition is addressed. And, if you have some time, inform them and even recruit them to help gather more signatures.

Petitioning may be inexpensive but it can be very time consuming. A lot of people may be needed over a significant period of time to secure a critical mass of signatures.

Canvassing. Canvassing is the act of going door to door to contact people. Several of our teams discovered that they could get a good deal accomplished when canvassing: publicize a meeting, recruit volunteers, gather opinions, get signatures on a petition, promote political candidates, and so forth. Some of our students focused on nuisance crimes associated with liquor stores. They were surprised to learn through canvassing that most of the residents in the area did not have any complaints about nuisance crimes associated with local liquor stores, contrary to what the students had expected.

Like petitioning, canvassing is usually inexpensive but time consuming. It is best done in small geographical areas. Canvassing can be quite rewarding. Student citizens often enjoy meeting and speaking with people. Like telephoning, however, be prepared to encounter people who feel that you are intruding on their time, space, or privacy. As soon as you see that they do not want to listen or talk to you, move on. Always be polite. Always thank them for giving you their time.

Surveys. Surveys are a great way to take "the public pulse." They can reveal people's opinions of candidates, their views on particular issues, and their suggestions for improvement. Surveys also can help you to assess the impact of various policies on the people most directly affected by them.

Surveys can be administered in several ways: on the telephone, through the mail, or by way of in-person interviews. Make certain that your survey is as brief as possible. Ask yourself, "What do I want to learn from this survey?" Develop questions that are directly focused on your key concerns. Avoid the temptation to include extraneous questions. Avoid asking "leading" questions such as, "Do you approve of the clean ocean campaign or do you think the evil factory owners should be allowed to dump poisonous waste into the oceans where our children swim?"

Before administering a survey, select your target population. Are you interested in the opinions of commuter students, or minority residents of a particular neighborhood, or people who regularly ride on public transportation? Once you select your target population, determine the best way for you to contact a "sample" or subset of that population. Be creative. For example, if your target population is commuter students, have team members bring clipboards, surveys, and pencils to campus parking lots during the morning rush and evening exodus. You cannot survey everyone but you may be able to survey a strong sample of commuter students.

Public Meetings and Film Screenings. Public meetings and film screenings provide you the opportunity to promote two-way communication between you, your team, or your partner organization and the public. You can express your ideas and provide audience members an opportunity to express their views.

To prepare the audience for an honest and open discussion, it is often a good idea to have an appropriate speaker or to screen a relevant film to impart information, raise questions, and stimulate thought and conversation about the issue that concerns you. Sometimes, it is useful to conduct surveys at meetings. Be advised that your sample may be quite different from the rest of the population. After all, your sample will exclude all people who were not willing or able to attend your meeting.

If you do decide to hold a public meeting, be prepared to devote much of your time to gathering an audience. Do you have a topic, or speaker, or film that will draw people in? How will you inform them about the meeting? Do you plan to remind them as the meeting time draws near? Is the meeting place easily accessible? Is the meeting day and time convenient for your potential audience? Have you planned the meeting on a day when other events (for example, the Superbowl) are attracting people's attention?

Letter Writing Campaigns. Legislators usually pay close attention to the opinions of their constituents. While they do not read every letter they receive, their aides usually keep a tally of the opinions expressed in letters. One way to get your voice heard in legislative circles, then, is to organize a letter writing campaign.

Ideally, you will recruit a significant number of people who are constituents of the targeted legislator to write their own personalized letters to express the common concerns of your team or organization. Legislators generally give more weight to letters from constituents than outsiders. Furthermore, they tend to discount the significance of the message when they receive a large pile of signed "form letters."

Another way to get your voice heard is by writing letters to the editor of local newspapers. Remember to be clear and concise. Newspapers have significant space constraints and tend to publish short letters rather than long ones.

Boycotts. A boycott is an effort to refuse to patronize or cooperate with a store or organization in an effort to change its behavior. For example, Civil Rights activists in the 1950s and 1960s organized campaigns to get consumers to stop patronizing businesses that refused to serve African Americans, hire African Americans, or treat African Americans with respect. Their hope was that the loss of revenue would persuade store owners to act more justly.

When launching a boycott, keep two things in mind. First, a major effort will be needed to publicize a boycott and an even greater effort will be required to win people's cooperation. Second, you should let the business or organization that you are boycotting know who is boycotting them, why they are being boycotted, and what they can do to prevent or end the boycott. Again, check campus or city regulations to be sure that your boycott does not run afoul of local rules or laws.

Picketing. Picketing can be an effective way to attract attention to an issue. People marching up and down sidewalks, carrying large signs proclaiming their causes, chanting slogans and singing songs—all of this has an audio and visual dimension that can attract the attention of local residents as well as the print and broadcast media.

Picketing tends to be an "in-your-face" technique, a way for people "to speak truth to power." The downside is that it can easily become confrontational. Furthermore, people who live or work in the area are often disturbed when picketers block sidewalks, cause traffic slowdowns, and create unwanted congestion.

Many jurisdictions have laws that restrict picketing. For example, a permit may be required. Some rules may be strictly enforced. Learn the rules so that you will be able to generate publicity for your cause without alienating potential supporters or having the authorities cut short your demonstration.

The Media. You may want to get your voice heard on a large scale. Your options include radio and television call-in shows, free editorial time on news broadcasts, public service announcements, and cable access stations. The broadcast media afford you an opportunity to get your message to a great many people.

If you want to reach other students, find out if your school has a television station, radio station, or newspaper. Note that both the broadcast and print media generally offer free announcements or free listings of upcoming events. One of our student teams sponsored a community meeting. It broadcast a free public service announcement about the meeting and persuaded a student reporter to do a story on the meeting. The team got front-page coverage!

Choosing Tactics

When choosing which tactics are right for you, ask yourself several questions. First and foremost, "Does this tactic fit into my game plan?" Or, "Will it help me achieve my goals?" If your game plan calls for raising general public awareness about the environment, it would probably be better for you to spend your time seeking access to the media rather than to canvass door-to-door in a large area. On the other hand, if your goal is to get a campus restaurant to charge fairer prices to students, canvassing dormitories might be an effective tactic for building support.

Next, ask yourself, "Does this tactic complement any other tactic that might be helpful?" For instance, distributing flyers and setting up an information table work well together. The flyers are food for further thought for those who stop by your table and the table provides you an appropriate audience to receive your flyers. Be conscious about coordinating your tactics. It will enhance your effectiveness.

A third question for consideration is, "Would I be good at this tactic?" Try to choose tactics that draw on your personal strengths (and those of other team members). If you are relatively shy, you may decide that you would be better at developing a web site than at doing door-to-door canvassing. If you consider yourself a "people person," the opposite choice might suit you.

Then ask yourself, "Do I have the resources to use this tactic?" Some tactics cost money. Some require transportation. Other tactics take a lot of time. Still others demand specific skills. Choose those tactics that are affordable and doable.

Now consider this question: "Can I work with other individuals, groups, or organizations so that this tactic will be more successful?" A bit of research may uncover dozens of organized groups already working on your issue. See if you can cooperate with them. Conceivably, these groups can help you with organizing events, canvassing a neighborhood, providing mailing lists, or even photocopying written materials. Be prepared for some give and take: they may expect you to assist them in a letter writing campaign or some other tactic.

A final question is, "Will this tactic make me appear to be unreasonable or pushy?" This is important. People are apt to be more receptive to your information and ideas if you avoid presenting yourself as a "know-it-all" from the college. Instead, present yourself as a thoughtful person who has concerns that you wish to discuss with other people.

Questions to Ask Yourself When Choosing Tactics

• Does this tactic fit my goals and game plan?

• Does this tactic complement other tactics?

• Would I be good at this?

• Do I have the resources to pursue it?

• Can I work with other individual or groups to be more successful with it?

• Will this tactic make me seem thoughtful and concerned?

These questions do not provide you with precise rules for what you should or should not do. Every student project and political endeavor is somewhat unique. Nonetheless, we hope these questions provide you with some general guidance about the factors you should consider when selecting tactics. Think of it this way. When you are assessing a particular tactic, if you can give a positive answer to all of the questions above, you can feel confident that you have made a good selection.

Working With Allies 6

Flexibility, Dependability, Civility,
and Perseverance

You or your team may benefit from getting connected with other individuals, groups, or organizations on your campus or in your community. Most of our teams had partner organizations that expanded options, improved access to resources, and provided insight into politics. There is a trade-off. Working with allies can make your group more effective but it also links you to people who have their own goals, game plans, and tactical preferences.

One major challenge involved in collaborating with partners is that you must work with people you do not know. You are already busy with commitments outside of your project. Now, your allies may have fairly demanding ideas about how much you should work, when, where, and how. For alliances to be fruitful, both you and your partners need to exhibit considerable flexibility, dependability, civility, and perseverance.

Flexibility

Flexibility is crucial to building successful alliances. It is one thing to develop your own goals, game plans, and tactics. But it is quite another to know whether to adjust, alter, or replace them as it becomes apparent that they are not working well, or that there is a better option, or that your allies have different ideas about how to proceed. Do not wed yourself to early decisions if you plan to affiliate with another organization, such as a political campaign or a neighborhood organization. Keep your options open.

Why? The good news is that established organizations are likely to have far more experience than you, superior knowledge of the issues and players, a better sense of workable tactics, and an interest in helping students to understand the politics of the local arena. If you are flexible and open to suggestions from your allies, you will probably learn a good deal. Some of our most successful student teams made major changes in their game plans and tactics because they felt they would be more successful by following their more experienced allies' advice.

The bad news, of course, is that you and your team gain the benefit of others' experience by sacrificing a degree of autonomy. Sometimes, you will have to set aside your own desires to satisfy your partner. You may even feel as if you are being treated like an empty-headed subordinate. If so, talk to your allies. Let them know your feelings, preferences, and reasoning. Seek to negotiate and compromise your differences.

The degree of control that you or your team retains over the project depends in part on the type of organization with which you ally. If you are joining a political campaign or collaborating with a well-established organization, the chances are strong that your control will be minimal. You may find yourself reporting to a coordinator or supervisor who simply assigns tasks to you.

Nonetheless, this can be a marvelous learning experience. You can glimpse the inner workings of a political organization and be a part of it. You may not be able to choose your own goals, game plan, or tactics, but you may be compensated by the exhilaration of being involved in something substantial and important.

We had several teams allied with campaign organizations. They usually found themselves doing whatever their supervisors requested at the moment. They staffed phone banks, registered voters, canvassed neighborhoods, and attended political events. A number of them were rewarded with fairly unique experiences. One student met the President of the United States.

An alternative to allying with a large political organization is to get involved with a community group concerned with local issues such as trying to get a stop sign put in at a busy intersection. Involvement with community groups might be less alluring than national political campaigns. It will provide you little opportunity to meet famous leaders. But it does provide two advantages.

First, you should be able to protect your autonomy when allying with a neighborhood organization. Welcome to the world of amateur politics where no one is quite sure how things work and everyone is looking to clarify goals, construct reasonable game plans, and experiment with workable tactics. Your ideas and recommendations are likely to get a better hearing because your allies are likely to be fairly flexible about how to proceed.

Second, you may be able to achieve a strong sense of accomplishment by allying with a local group. If you are examining the possibilities of a street closure near a school or trying to ensure affordable rents for local seniors, you may be able to enhance the quality of life for a few people in a small corner of your community and do it in a relatively short period of time.

Dependability

Dependability counts . . . a lot! This is especially true when you are working with a relatively small group in which every individual's contribution is essential to the successful achievement of goals. Dependability is also important when working with large organizations that must coordinate the activities of many people. If one person does not do his or her job as planned, others may not be able to complete their tasks.

One of our student teams ran into a major problem when one student proved to be undependable. The team was working with a local grocer to determine the best way to keep shopping carts from being abandoned in the neighborhood. Crucial to this student-grocer alliance was a student who spoke Korean, because the Korean grocer spoke almost no English. When this student failed to show up for meetings, the team was unable to communicate with its ally.

When working with allies, you are representing yourself, your team, and your school. Be dependable. If you say you will be somewhere at a particular time, be there on time. Do not expect others to cover for you.

Being dependable is even more important when working with people in the community who may have much more than a class grade at stake. Do not make promises to them that you cannot keep. Follow through on your commitments. Behave in a way that will allow other students to continue to make alliances with community groups.

Our student teams sometimes encountered resentment in the community surrounding our university. The source of resentment was that students in the past had worked with community groups but proved to be irresponsible. By contrast, our most responsible student teams paved the way for future students to enter into community politics with the friendly presumption that they will be dependable colleagues, not burdensome pests.

Dependability is a two-way street. There are problems if you are not dependable. But there are also problems if your allied organization does not follow through. We had several student teams that experienced frustration when their partners acted irresponsibly. Be aware that this happens for several reasons.

Your allies may not have their act together. They might lack clarity or coherence in their own goals, game plans, and tactics. Perhaps they are poorly organized and lacking effective leadership. They may have taken on more than they can handle and some things, such as your alliance, fall by the wayside. Most likely, your allies are dealing with other, more pressing matters, such as a budget crisis or programmatic difficulties. A well-meaning contact person may have put your partnership on the back burner.

Another reason that your allies may be undependable involves their assumptions about college students. They may feel that college students are not a priority because they are not an enduring part of the organization. Your contact people may not be quite sure about what to do with you or your team. They may be wary about your motivations and abilities. Maybe they resent the fact that their superiors assigned you to them.

If your partners prove to be undependable, you may have to take more initiative than you expected. Brainstorm your options. Can you figure a way to coordinate more effectively with your allies? If you take more responsibility for a joint project, will your partner organization be more likely to make some contribution to the effort? What can you do to demonstrate that students do have the motivation and ability to contribute to common goals? We suggest that "doing nothing" is not an option.

One of our student-citizen teams worked with a community organization to improve and beautify the environment by planting trees on school grounds. Unfortunately, the students' contact person sent them to schools that did not exist or that were unaware that anyone was supposed to plant trees on their premises. After three or four unsuccessful attempts, the team nearly quit. But it didn't. The students communicated the problem to the community organization and received guarantees that the next planting would go better. Thereafter, a few tree-planting events did proceed as planned.

Civility

A crucial skill to master when working with allied groups is civility—the ability to maintain cordial, collegial relationships even when you find yourself in disagreement with others. Civility has three great advantages in politics.

First, civility is a strategy for being effective. Other people are more likely to respect you, listen to you, and even be persuaded by you if they feel that you treat them with due respect. Benjamin Franklin suggested that civility makes you a better companion and makes your arguments more worthy of attention, if not agreement. Thomas Jefferson added that a little politeness is a small price to pay to gain other people's esteem and cooperation.

Second, civility keeps open your options for collaboration. When you and your allies disagree, civility enables you to focus discussion on disputed ideas rather than personalities. Accordingly, you can keep the discussion going and keep alive the possibilities for negotiation, compromise, and continuing partnership.

Third, in politics, today's ally and today's opponent may be tomorrow's partners. It is foolish to engage in mean-spirited behavior with your allies if only because you may want to work with them on a different project in the future. Do not burn bridges.

Let us mention one more advantage of civility: it helps to get you through hard times. We believe that many of our student teams were able to experience significant success because they maintained an atmosphere of civility amidst adversity. When things did not go smoothly, these students refused to blame each other or their allies. Instead, they tried to transform each frustration into a problem that needed to be addressed.

Perseverance

You may encounter unforeseen challenges that test your ability to follow through on promises or keep an alliance intact. For example, transportation can become a major issue if only one team member has an automobile. Try to plan road trips that accommodate that car owner's schedule. Or have several team members explore the city's transportation system. Another possibility is to seek a new ally that is closer to your school.

One of our teams allied with an organization that was thirty miles from our campus. The students had to attend periodic meetings at the organization's headquarters but only one team member had a car. With a bit of effort, a lot of good will, and a commitment to persevere, other team members gently persuaded the car owner to alter his social schedule to accommodate team needs.

With tight class schedules, some team members may be unable to participate in events scheduled by your team (which you probably can control) or by your partner organization (which you probably cannot control). This should not be a serious problem. One of our student citizens put it this way:

> We completely understood if people couldn't make it to every event or every meeting. I don't think we had everyone there more than two or three times. We all had other classes to worry about and other responsibilities to work around. We all understood that if you couldn't make it to the event that you should try to make sure you made it to the next one that would come up in the next week or so. I think it worked out pretty well.

Another team had more difficult scheduling conflicts. One student was on the school football team. Another student was a middle-aged, family man with a full-time job. Several students had majors, academic interests, and social cares that had little to do with politics. Initially, this team accomplished little. No one contacted the allied organization. After a few weeks, however, two students emerged as leaders, worked out a division of labor, did most of the team conferencing by telephone and e-mail, and became liaisons between the team and its partner. Initiative and perseverance enabled the team and its ally to achieve their joint goal.

The amount of time that you and other students spend on your project will likely be quite small in comparison to the time commitment made by your allied organization. Nonetheless, you may find that there are moments when your portion of the project seems to be at a standstill. This is likely during times when you are waiting for phone calls to be returned, or team members are studying for mid-term exams, or scheduling conflicts grow worse than ever. Nothing seems to be getting done. During periods of inactivity, remind yourself that patience is important. Also, it is okay to fall short of your goals but it is not okay to give up on them.

We had a few students (fortunately, a very few) who simply dropped out of their projects because they felt overwhelmed or they did not see their projects going anywhere. Don't let this be you. If you have a bad week, figure that the next one will be better. If you let the team down, make it up to them. If your allies have not returned your phone calls, call them back. Do not let the difficulties pile up.

One of our student citizens described his team's experience with drop-outs this way:

> I think one of our members just gave up. He hung out with us for a couple of weeks but then we just never saw him again. The thing was, he didn't need to give up. We weren't mad at him. We all had bad weeks, but I think he just thought we'd get all over him for not contacting us and he just gave up. That's too bad.

How do you avoid this experience? One useful method for getting through "bad weeks" is to plan ahead. Look at your calendar and anticipate weeks when you will have to devote your energies to other responsibilities. Have your team members sit down, compare calendars, and decide who might be able to bear more of the load one week so he or she will have more time to study for exams the next week. Bring your calendar with you when meeting with your partner organization. See if you can plan meetings and events to accommodate both of your schedules.

Above all else, persevere! You, your team, and your allies
usually can work out difficulties if you keep at it. And even if you
cannot resolve some problems, you can learn from the experience.
Politics is not only about working with other people and
organizations; it is also about the problems that make working with
other people and organizations challenging.

Working With Others

• *Flexibility*: Nothing about your project is set in stone.
Keep an eye on your main goals. Think about what you
want to accomplish. Be prepared to modify your game plan
when working with other people and organizations.

• *Dependability*: Follow through with your promises. The
most effective teams are composed of responsible students
who do their fair share. The most successful projects are
based on the mutual responsibility exhibited by student
teams and allied organizations.

• *Civility*: Your ideas will be taken more seriously if you
express your views in ways that respect the ideas of other
people, even people who disagree with you. Civility in
the face of adversity demonstrates your political maturity
and willingness to compromise to achieve your goals.

• *Perseverance*: Every team has a down time. Even with
good planning and scheduling, participants in politics
encounter unexpected obstacles when working with other
people and organizations. Know that problems arise and
persevere in your efforts to solve them.

Learning From Others

It can be intimidating to walk into the offices of a large,
established organization. It may be uncomfortable speaking to a
seasoned political veteran about engaging in a project of mutual
interest. Still, we think this is an invaluable experience. It initiates
you into the culture of politics and public service. One of our
students noted, "We had to get used to a professional atmosphere.
They talk in a certain way, do certain things, and hold themselves in
a certain manner. I feel like I can pull it off now."

It also can be intimidating to work in a community made up of people who are significantly different from you because of race, class, religion, or education. Maybe local residents have different values than you. Perhaps they see politics differently than you. They may even be suspicious of you because of your skin color or your association with the college. Again, we think this can be a valuable experience. Higher education teaches you to understand the world, if not experience it, from many points of view, even if you do not agree with them. Politics demands that you learn to work with diverse people to build effective coalitions, win elections, or make laws and policies for a heterogeneous population.

One of the great thrills of political participation is that it challenges you to reach beyond your own private life to become a part of a rich and complex public world. One of the great advantages of participating on a team and working with allies is that you are apt to encounter and learn from experienced professionals who can help situate you in the public sphere.

Overcoming Obstacles   7

Free Riders, Miscommunication,
Overconfidence, and Rigidity

Ideally, you will achieve your goals by following your game plan and employing your tactics in conjunction with your allies. Of course, something could go wrong. It is generally wise to anticipate common obstacles in order to prevent or overcome them.

Many of the obstacles considered here appear when you are an individual intern working within an organization, a team member collaborating with other team members, or part of a team that allies itself with a partner organization. We conclude with an example of how one student team overcame several significant obstacles to achieve success.

Free Riders

A student intern working with people in an established organization, a team of students working on a political project, or a group alliance united for a specific purpose depend on each other to achieve shared goals. When one or more people fail to fulfill their responsibilities, everyone else suffers the consequences.

One common group occurrence is the "free-rider" problem. As we explained in Chapter 3, a free rider is someone who does little or nothing to contribute to a group's efforts but still expects to receive credit for the group's accomplishments. A student may fail to show up for team meetings, ignore his tasks, rely on others to fill in, but still expect the same grade as every other team member.

Often it is difficult to spot a free rider at the beginning of a team project. But warning signs are usually telling. Free riders often show a lack of enthusiasm. They are reticent to volunteer, except for parts of the project that require the least amount of work. They may complain about how busy they already are, as if no one else's time matters. At the outset, try to gauge individuals' enthusiasm and commitment to ensure that everyone knows they are expected to do their fair share. You may choose to talk about the free-rider problem in the hope of avoiding it.

Usually, a little support from other team members is enough to change a person's attitude. If you suspect someone is likely to become a free rider, both encourage his participation and protect the project by giving him responsibilities that are not vital to the team. Your encouragement may help him to fulfill his responsibilities whereas your criticism could alienate him and make the problem worse. Meanwhile, if he proves to be a free rider, at least the team will be able to continue with its game plan.

When a free rider does emerge, all group members should be made aware of the problem. Rather than accuse the free rider of failing the team, express your concerns, talk about consequences for the team, and give the free rider an opportunity to make up his work. You may be able to bring him back into the fold.

Another way to deal with a free rider is for team members to put pressure on him to do his job. Coordinate your efforts with other team members. Remind your free rider of the need for teamwork. Stress the significance of his tasks. Let him know that everyone is counting on him. The pressure should be gentle. If it appears that everyone is "ganging up" on him, he may disappear.

When all else fails, inform your professor of the problem. It is preferable if you ask her advice about ways to solve the problem rather than to depend on her to solve it. An important challenge in democratic politics is to win the cooperation of people who fail to do their civic duty. You need to learn how to deal with it.

Miscommunication

In today's high-tech world of e-mail, voice mail, fax machines, and cellular phones, the human factor still determines the clarity and coherence of communication. Interns, teams, and allies must communicate with each other to coordinate joint efforts. Any miscommunication may result in time wasted, missed assignments and appointments, and the alienation of partners and supporters.

Begin with the assumption that everyone is busy and involved in many things besides your political project. Your phone calls may go unanswered. People may return them when you are out. Be prepared to play "phone tag." And persevere. Try alternative means of communication. Try e-mail or a fax machine.

When scheduling meetings or appointments, make sure that everyone has advanced notice and agree to a specific time, date, and place. If you must cancel and reschedule, do so as far in advance as possible. If you will miss a meeting, let others know.

Often, people do not understand what is expected of them. They may not say anything or ask questions because they do not want to sound dumb. When you meet with collaborators, encourage questions, restate responsibilities, and review the division of labor.

If you are conducting the meeting, be sure that individuals are apprised not only of their own work but of everyone's work.

Openness is crucial. If someone makes a mistake, foster an atmosphere in which people feel comfortable to admit it, learn from it, and correct it. When people expect blame, they are less likely to be open about a problem. It may fester and grow worse.

When working with the public, government officials, or people from allied organizations, be forthright about your motives, intentions, and desires. For instance, tell people that you are a college student engaged in a class project. You may find that people will be more willing to help you because they value education.

Practice honesty and exhibit professionalism to build bonds of trust between you and others. If people think you are deceiving them, they will not want to work with you. If you cannot maintain a relatively calm, reasonable demeanor, they may doubt your reliability and intelligence. Practice civility, particularly when dealing with "the other side." Earn your opponents' respect. You may end up working with them one day.

Try not to personalize uncomfortable incidents. You should not feel insulted, for example, if you speak to someone for the third time but they do not remember you. Do not get defensive if someone from an allied group misses an appointment. People juggle many concerns. They have multiple priorities. They forget things. Try to be understanding and tolerant.

Overconfidence

Overconfidence can be the source of two serious obstacles to success. First, it can weaken alliances and estrange potential supporters. We have many white students from affluent families working in low-income, minority neighborhoods near our school. An occasional student takes the attitude that he is some kind of Moses sent to set free poor people. This is a major mistake.

The source of overconfidence is often fear. A young person who has led a sheltered life in wealthy suburbs may fear going into a low-income, minority neighborhood where people seem to look and act differently. Big talk may shield him from fear but it also shields him from learning about himself and diverse people. On the other hand, a student who has survived the "mean streets" and made it to college may have a superior attitude and overestimate how much college status ensures her credibility with community leaders.

Residents of low-income neighborhoods (especially those near universities) have encountered their share of overconfident college kids who spend a few weeks trying to save the neighborhood. They see the students as transients who come and go while they remain settled. Residents often develop a healthy skepticism of know-it-all students who talk big but accomplish little. The swaggering student who seeks to work with residents is almost certain to receive a cold if not hostile reception.

Consider the virtues of modesty. Listen to people. Learn from them. Above all else, do not tell them what to do. Rather, build sufficient trust so that you can work with them.

Second, overconfidence may upset working relations in your internship or on your team. When people are overconfident in their solutions to problems, they tend to insulate themselves from other ideas, useful criticisms, and troublesome evidence. Do not think that just because you have studied a problem and designed a good game plan that it will necessarily work. It may, but it may not.

Keep asking yourself if there is a second, third, or fourth alternative that merits consideration. Invite criticism from team members and collaborators. They may see things that you are missing. Consider potential obstacles. What can go wrong? What is likely to go wrong? Who might resist your efforts?

Ultimately, you must strike a balance. When you have chosen goals, designed a game plan, selected tactics, and built alliances, you should feel confident enough to carry out your plan. Still, remember there are other plans and allies that reasonable folks might consider more promising. Be confident but be open to ideas and information that invite you to rethink and refine your plans.

Rigidity

Sometimes, things go wrong midway through a project. You may feel a strong temptation toward rigidity. You may want to stick to your original goals, plans, tactics, and alliances as if nothing has happened. Rigidity is tempting. You can pretend nothing is wrong. You can wait until someone else figures out what to do. Our advice is: Resist temptation.

Be prepared for things to go wrong. After you have made your major decisions, do a "worst-case scenario" exercise. Give consideration to these questions, "What is the worst thing that can happen during this project? What can we do to prevent it or mitigate likely consequences?"

We had two teams that organized public meetings. Their worst-case scenario was that nobody would show up. Accordingly, they put the bulk of their energy into publicizing the events, issuing invitations, calling people to remind them as the events drew near, and, in one case, getting up at 6 A.M. to place announcement signs all over campus on the day of the meeting. If you prepare for the worst, you usually can avoid it.

Another way to prepare for problems is to design a game plan that invites you to use multiple tactics. This is a version of "don't put all your eggs in one basket." One tactic may not work well. It might take too much time. It may require too much reliance on one person. Be adaptable. Refocus your energy into another tactic that is likely to work as well if not better than the original.

Develop a contingency plan. Imagine alternative game plans to achieve your goals. Ponder the possibility of different tactics. We had one team that found setting up a table in a high-pedestrian area was ineffective. Hardly anyone stopped at their table. Halfway through their project, they shifted tactics and decided to canvass a nearby neighborhood. Canvassing proved to be a more effective way to distribute their materials.

You also can develop a contingency plan for internal team problems. If something happened to prevent any one member of your team from participating, would you have the capacity to cover for him or her? If you divide team labor not among individuals but among pairs, you can avoid becoming too dependent on any one person. Meanwhile, your alliances may be helpful if you need to shore up your team with extra personnel or expertise.

Do not be surprised to encounter unanticipated obstacles. Student citizens are political amateurs who cannot predict the future. Even political professionals cannot control all twists and turns in politics. Be sufficiently flexible to recognize and correct your mistakes, find ways to work with others, and revise goals, game plans, tactics, and alliances when necessary.

Political Troubleshooting

• Beware of free riders.

• Encourage everyone to do his or her fair share.

• Keep open the lines of communication.

• Be confident, not overconfident.

• Avoid rigidity. Be flexible.

• Prepare for the unexpected.

A Case Study in Adversity

If you ignore problems, they may snowball. If you confront them, you probably can overcome most obstacles. Here is the story of one team of student citizens who confronted adversity.

One of our student teams decided to address the problem of shopping cart theft in a local neighborhood. Shopping carts were being taken from store premises by shoppers who used them to transport groceries home and by homeless people who carried their life's belongings in them.

The stolen carts cost grocers thousands of dollars each year. Grocers covered losses by raising prices charged to consumers. Residents complained that abandoned shopping carts littered the neighborhood. They also worried that homeless people wheeled them around as a pretense for casing homes for possible burglary.

Our student citizens brainstormed goals, game plans, and tactics. They decided to study the problem of shopping cart theft, propose solutions to it, and persuade a nearby chain grocery store to implement their recommendations.

Much to their surprise and annoyance, the manager of the chain store was not interested in the team's research or proposals. But because the team tailored its efforts to address this one store's needs, it was at a loss about what to do next.

The students decided to contact a neighborhood organization to better understand the problem. The students finally reached a representative of the organization only to learn that it had an entirely different view of the problem.

Originally, our team thought that it needed to balance the interests of the grocery store owners (minimizing their losses) and nearby residents (finding ways to transport groceries home). However, the neighborhood organization's main concern was to restrict access to the shopping carts in order to drive homeless people away from the area. The students ultimately decided that they could not work with this neighborhood organization.

Exhibiting perseverance and flexibility, they contacted the owner of another nearby market and discussed their ideas with him. They received a more positive response from a small, local market than the larger, chain store operation. Even with the added problem of a free rider, the team was able to develop a set of policy recommendations and present it to the owner for implementation.

This example is instructive. The team was able to modify its game plan and tactics each time a new problem emerged. Furthermore, the students probably learned more from their project (and got a good grade for it) than students on other teams whose projects went far more smoothly.

Making a Difference 8

Payoffs, Change, and Success

You have gotten connected, fostered teamwork, set goals, designed game plans, employed tactics, built alliances, and overcome obstacles. Now, what can you hope to accomplish in a few months? Is it possible for you to make a difference in your own life, on your campus, in the community, and at the national level? Yes it is!

Individual Payoffs

The biggest payoff from your political involvement may be the difference it makes in your own life. Student citizenship may offer you concrete advantages and new options.

Let us be practical. A record of public service is an asset for your résumé when applying for admission to graduate or professional education or when you are searching for a job. Also, it may provide interesting anecdotes to relate during interviews.

Consider your participation an opportunity to network with influential people. If you earn their respect for your effort, intelligence, and performance, you may be able to call on them to write letters of recommendation, give you part-time work, introduce you to potential employers, or even offer you a full-time job.

Student citizenship provides you opportunities to develop practical skills that may affect your future. For example, once you learn that researching an organization's needs is useful for negotiating your project, you should recognize that researching a potential employer's goals in preparation for a job interview may improve your chances for success.

When you master the art of civility to work with diverse people, communities, and organizations, you also prepare yourself to build fruitful working relations with the diverse people who will be neighbors, supervisors, colleagues, competitors, and clients later in life. Student citizenship skills are adult living skills, too.

Some students find that getting involved in politics changes their lives. We had a team of students who worked to elect several

California Democrats. When assessing their experience, the students emphasized the project's affect on them:

> Our work on the campaign may not have changed the flow of the election, but it truly influenced us. We were all exposed to a side of politics that we had never seen. Most of us have decided to work on campaigns this summer. Some of us are going to try to work on the local level, others at the state, while some wish to intern in Washington, D.C.

We suspect that several students changed their career trajectories as a result of getting involved in politics.

Changing the World

You have heard the saying, "Think globally, act locally." You can make a difference on global issues by participating in local politics. Your participation in formulating an anti-racist code of ethics, or your efforts to tutor youths with learning disabilities, or your work with a human rights commission can make a contribution to the cause of building greater harmony and unity among diverse peoples on campus, in the neighborhood, and beyond.

That was how the Civil Rights Movement got started. Local community organizing in the 1940s set the stage for the civil rights activism that swept across the southern United States in the 1950s, assumed national dimensions in the 1960s, and fostered global efforts in the decades that followed.

One of our student teams decided to start a Human Rights Watch (HRW) chapter on campus. Its goal was to organize a local chapter, publicize it, build its membership, and raise campus awareness of human rights issues and violations. However, as one student put it, the team's project got "hijacked" when a group of graduate students declared themselves the HRW leaders on campus.

Our students were sufficiently flexible to work with the graduate students. They also revised their project. They researched and set up a campus web site that provided information about the organization, listed campus courses that dealt with human rights issues, and promoted discussion about human rights abuses. When the project ended, the students concluded that their efforts had helped to create a viable campus presence "that could better serve college students concerned with human rights." Several students continued to work with the organization on their own.

Of course these student citizens did not end human rights abuses. But they became a part of the solution. Their local activism in conjunction with the efforts of many, many other citizens may eventually add up to regional, national, and even global change.

The Meaning of Political Success

Here are three important lessons about the meaning of political success in America. First, citizen efforts to influence law and public policy go on and on. Citizens achieve no final victories; citizens suffer no final losses. Today's success may be tomorrow's failure, and vice versa. Second, citizens rarely succeed or fail per se; they usually achieve partial victories and experience partial defeats. Third, politics is not always about winning and losing. It is often about people working together to improve their lives. Participation, cooperation, and improvement all constitute political success.

Student citizens will not solve enduring social problems or right major political wrongs in just a few weeks. However, if you carry on earlier efforts, you are successful in keeping an issue alive. If you work to reverse old losses or transform half victories into whole ones, you are successful in reaffirming the right of your generation to govern itself. If you bequeath an activist legacy for others to take up in the future, you are successful in laying the groundwork for future collaborative efforts. Success in American politics is a matter of carrying on, maintaining, and bequeathing.

Let us provide some examples. When students work to get candidates elected, they carry on, maintain, and bequeath a long-standing tradition of citizen voluntarism. They freely give their time to participate in electoral politics and help their preferred candidates to win public office. Suppose that all of their candidates lose the election. Have these students been successful?

One of our student teams worked for major Republican candidates in California. All of their candidates lost their races. Here is how team members evaluated their accomplishments:

> We made a great contribution to the Republican party. We reminded many, many people to make sure to vote. We gave voting information to many, and may have even persuaded a few to vote Republican. Even though none of our candidates won, we felt that we did help the party and directly affected the election by getting people to vote. By helping the party and increasing the vote, we directly influenced politics in this state.

These students recognized that they made a difference even though their candidates lost. They carried on a tradition of political

voluntarism, helped to maintain the strength of their party, and even won a few converts to it.

Another student team sought to carry on, maintain, and bequeath the memory of Robert F. Kennedy (who was assassinated in 1968 while campaigning for the Democratic nomination for the presidency). They helped to launch a new organization—the RFK Forum—devoted to perpetuating Kennedy's commitment to youth education, civic participation, and social justice. The students' game plan was to attract people to the organization's inaugural event. They sent out invitations. They publicized the speakers by staffing phone banks, distributing flyers, posting signs, and contacting the media. Their efforts paid off. The inaugural event attracted significant interest, attendance, and publicity.

Nonetheless, our student citizens were a bit disappointed. Their belief was that this was an event that "should not be missed by any politically-minded young person." They were frustrated that the event did not turn out to be a "standing room only" affair. Their frustration was understandable. The students wanted to make a difference by generating massive enthusiasm. Their achievement fell somewhat short of that goal.

Fortunately, team members understood and appreciated the fact that their efforts contributed to a successful first step toward what was likely to be a long-term political endeavor. Much to our delight, another team of student citizens decided to continue their efforts by working with the RFK Forum the next semester.

•••••

Getting involved in politics is an important means to learn about American politics, practice it, and participate in it. Your involvement may be frustrating at times, but it can be immensely gratifying, too. We have written this booklet to help you to reduce the frustrations and fully enjoy the rewards of student citizenship.